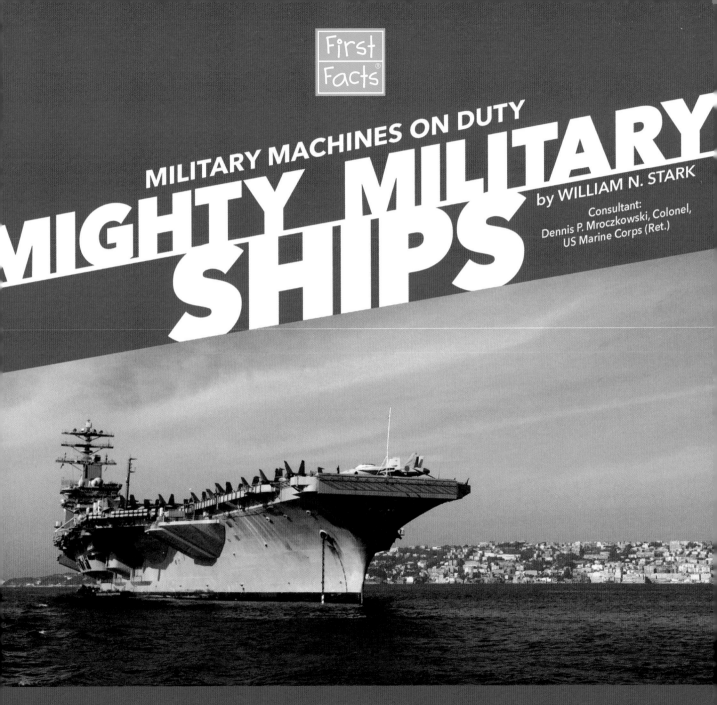

First Facts®

MILITARY MACHINES ON DUTY

MIGHTY MILITARY SHIPS

by WILLIAM N. STARK

Consultant:
Dennis P. Mroczkowski, Colonel,
US Marine Corps (Ret.)

CAPSTONE PRESS
a capstone imprint

First Facts are published by Capstone Press,
1710 Roe Crest Drive, North Mankato, Minnesota 56003
www.mycapstone.com

Library of Congress Cataloging-in-Publication Data
Stark, William N.
 Mighty military ships / by William N. Stark.
    pages cm. – (First facts. Military machines on duty)
 Includes bibliographical references and index.
 Summary: "Gives readers a quick look at modern military ships"– Provided by publisher.
 Audience: Grades K-3.
 ISBN 978-1-4914-8846-1 (hardcover)
 ISBN 978-1-4914-8850-8 (eBook PDF)
 1. Warships–United States–Juvenile literature. I. Title.
 VA58.4.W367 2016
 359.8'30973–dc23   2015029654

Editorial Credits: Mandy Robbins, editor; Kristi Carlson, designer;
Jo Miller, media researcher; Gene Bentdahl, production specialist

Photo Credits: U.S. Navy Photo by MC1 Jeffrey Jay Price, 7, MC1 Jennifer A. Villalovos, 21, (top), MC1 Trevor Welsh, 9, MC2 Jhi L. Scott, 21, (bottom), MC2 John Philip Wagner, Jr., Cover (top), 11, MC2 Justin Wolpert, Cover, (bottom), MC3 Johans Chavaro, 19, MC3 Kyle D. Gahlau, 5, MC3 Phil Ladouceur, 1, MCSN Brandon Myrick, 17, MCSN Christopher Frost, 12, PH3 Taylor Goode, 15,

Design Element: Shutterstock: Grebnev (metal texture background)

Printed in the United States of America in North Mankato, Minnesota
092015   009221CGS16

TABLE OF CONTENTS

RULING THE SEAS

Military ships display the United States' power. Before long-distance flight, they were the best way to move equipment, sailors, and Marines around the world. Ships continue to do this important work. They also provide support and protection for the United States. They help countries in need.

SUBMARINES

Submarines are airtight ships. They travel underwater and on the ocean's surface. Subs can attack enemy targets without being seen. The USS *Bremerton* is the oldest sub in the U.S. **fleet**. It is 360 feet (110 meters) long and holds 12 officers and 98 sailors. When it is **retired** in 2017, the ship will have served for 39 years.

fleet—a group of warships under one command
retire—to be taken out of the workforce

DESTROYERS

Destroyers can work alone or in a **carrier strike group**. They protect U.S. naval ships from attack. They also attack enemy targets onshore. The new Zumwalt-class destroyer cuts through waves. Its design helps it avoid enemy **radar**. The 610-foot (186-m) ship holds 186 people. These people care for the ship's weapons, radar, and aircraft.

FACT FILE

The U.S. military only uses three Zumwalt-class ships. The older Arleigh Burke-class ships make up the rest of the destroyers in the fleet.

carrier strike group—a group of military ships carrying out a mission together; typically made up of a carrier, a cruiser, a destroyer squadron, a submarine, and a supply ship

radar—a device that uses radio waves to track the location of objects

CRUISERS

Cruisers take on many types of missions. They take out targets at sea, on land, and in the air. Each one costs around $1 billion! The lead cruiser class is the Ticonderoga class. The U.S. has 22 of these ships in service. They are 567 feet (173 m) long and 55 feet (17 m) wide. Around 30 officers and 300 sailors operate a cruiser at sea.

Ticonderoga-class cruisers use the Aegis Combat System. In this system, electronic **sensors** control the ship's radar and weapons.

sensor—an instrument that detects physical changes in the environment

AIRCRAFT CARRIERS

The U.S. Navy has relied on aircraft carriers since the 1920s. This type of ship has a very large deck. Airplanes take off from and land on it. The largest of these ships are sometimes called supercarriers. They are more than 1,000 feet (305 m) long. They can hold up to 5,000 people. Supercarriers may carry more than 70 airplanes.

Testing on the USS *Gerald R. Ford* began in 2015. It is the first aircraft carrier of its class. The *Ford* will be armed with missiles and carry up to 90 aircraft.

AIRPLANES ON THE OCEAN

The first airplane flights lasted just seconds. Over time the distance an airplane could fly improved greatly. But airplanes still could not fly across oceans. They had to stop for fuel. Officers in the U.S. Navy realized that planes could be used from ships. That's why aircraft carriers became important.

AMPHIBIOUS ASSAULT SHIPS

Amphibious assault ships carry Marines and their equipment over water and onto land. The largest are the Tarawa-class LHAs and the Wasp-class LHDs. These ships look like small aircraft carriers. They quickly move Marines and equipment across oceans. LHAs and LHDs are used for both disaster relief and **combat** efforts.

FACT FILE

After Hurricane Katrina in 2005, LHD 7 served as the command center for rescue operations. It housed thousands of police and fire rescue workers near New Orleans.

combat—fighting between militaries

LANDING CRAFT

Landing craft move Marines and supplies from ships to shore. The LCAC looks like a giant raft. It carries up to 75 tons (68 metric tons) of **cargo**. The LCAC is about 92 feet (28 m) long and 48 feet (14.6 m) wide. LCMs and LCUs are hard-bottomed landing craft. Ramps let troops drive vehicles onto shore.

cargo—objects carried by a ship, aircraft, or other vehicle

knot—an international nautical unit of speed equal to 6,076 feet (1,852 m) per hour

LITTORAL COMBAT SHIPS

Littoral combat ships (LCS) are the navy's newest warships. LCSs are some of the fastest ships in the navy. They reach speeds of 40 knots. LCSs were built for missions in shallow coastal waters. They can also sail the open ocean. The first LCS, the USS *Freedom*, was **deployed** in 2010. Its crew went on four missions in three months.

deploy—to move troops into position for military action

AMAZING BUT TRUE!

Submarine sailors must pass three levels of advanced training. Sailors must remain calm in small spaces with no sunlight for long periods of time. They are tested to be sure they can do this. Sailors must also pass "pressure training." They learn breathing exercises to control the pressure in their ears. Last, sailors master challenging escape plans.

GLOSSARY

amphibious (*am-FI-bee-uhs*)—able to work on land or water

cargo (*KAR-go*)—objects carried by a ship, aircraft, or other vehicle

carrier strike group (*CARE-ee-ur STRYK GROOP*)—a group of military ships carrying out a mission together; typically made up of a carrier, a cruiser, a destroyer squadron, a submarine, and a supply ship

combat (*KOM-bat*)—fighting between militaries

deploy (*dih-PLOY*)—to move troops and equipment into position for military action

fleet (*FLEET*)—a group of warships under one command

knot (*NOT*)—an international nautical unit of speed equal to 6,076 feet (1,852 m) per hour

littoral (*lih-TORE-uhl*)—refers to shore or coastal area; littoral combat ships operate in the shallow waters of a coastline

radar (*RAY-dar*)—a device that uses radio waves to track the location of objects

retire (*rih-TIRE*)—to be taken out of the workforce

sensor (*SEN-sur*)—an instrument that detects physical changes in the environment

READ MORE

Alpert, Barbara. *Military Ships*. Military Machines. Mankato, Minn.: Capstone Press, 2012.

Nagelhout, Ryan. *Amphibious Vehicles*. Mighty Military Machines. New York: Gareth Stevens Publishing, 2015.

Nelson, Drew. *Submarines and Submersibles*. Military Machines. New York: Gareth Stevens Pub., 2013.

INTERNET SITES

FactHound offers a safe, fun way to find Internet sites related to this book. All of the sites on FactHound have been researched by our staff.

Here's all you do:

Visit *www.facthound.com*

Type in this code: 9781491488461

Check out projects, games and lots more at **www.capstonekids.com**

CRITICAL THINKING USING THE COMMON CORE

1. What benefits do you think a submarine might have in battle compared to a cruiser? (Key Ideas and Details)

2. Why might sailors be trained to control the pressure in their ears? (Integration of Knowledge and Ideas)

INDEX